old world swallowtail butterfly

Flutter, butterfly!

A butterfly lands on a plant.

butterfly

Pre-reader

Flutter, Butterfly!

Shelby Alinsky

NATIONAL GEOGRAPHIC

Washington, D.C.

VOCABULARY TREE

MY BACKYARD

ANIMALS

BUTTERFLY

WHAT IT DOES

lays an egg
hatches
crawls
eats
grows
changes
flutters

LIFE CYCLE

egg
caterpillar
pupa
butterfly

egg

It lays an egg.
The new egg is yellow.

Many days pass.
The egg turns brown.

A caterpillar grows
inside the egg.

Then the egg hatches!
The caterpillar comes out.

egg

The young caterpillar is black.

caterpillar

The caterpillar crawls
on plants.

It looks for food.
It eats leaves.

The caterpillar grows bigger.

It turns green.

The caterpillar keeps eating.

It eats more leaves.

After many weeks,

the caterpillar changes.

pupa

Now it's a pupa.

It's inside a hard covering.

Weeks pass.
A butterfly comes out!

butterfly

Flutter, butterfly!

Old World Swallowtail Life Cycle

egg

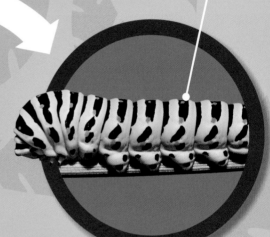

caterpillar

pupa

butterfly

YOUR TURN!

Match the word to the photo. Use your finger to make a line from the word to the photo.

EGG

BUTTERFLY

CATERPILLAR

PUPA

The answer is on the next page.

The publisher gratefully acknowledges the expert content review of this book by Dr. William O. Lamp, University of Maryland, Department of Entomology, and the expert literacy review by Susan B. Neuman, Ph.D., professor of early childhood and literacy education, New York University.

Trade paperback ISBN: 978-1-4263-2117-7
Reinforced library edition ISBN: 978-1-4263-2118-4

Project Editor: Shelby Alinsky
Series Editor: Shira Evans
Art Director: Callie Broaddus
Designer: Allie Allen
Photo Editor: Lori Epstein
Rights Clearance Specialist: Michael Cassady
Editorial Assistant: Paige Towler
Design Production Assistants: Sanjida Rashid and Rachel Kenny
Managing Editor: Grace Hill
Production Editor: Joan Gossett
Production Manager: Lewis R. Bassford
Manufacturing Manager: Rachel Faulise

Photo Credits
MP = Minden Pictures; NPL = Nature Picture Library
Cover, Katsuomi Matsumoto/Nature Production/MP; 1, blickwinkel/Alamy; 2-3, Jussi Murtosaari/NPL; 4, Terry Whittaker/2020VISION/NPL; 5, Silvia Reiche/MP; 6-7, Robert Pickett/Visuals Unlimited/Corbis; 8-9, Robert Pickett/Visuals Unlimited/Corbis; 10-11, Hans Christoph Kappel/NPL; 12-13, Flickr Open/Getty Images; 14, Silvia Reiche/MP; 15, Igor Semenov/Shutterstock; 16-17, Hans Christoph Kappel/NPL; 18-19, Hans Christoph Kappel/NPL; 20, Stephen Dalton/NPL; 21, Hans Christoph Kappel/NPL; 22 (egg), Silvia Reiche/MP; 22 (caterpillar, pupa, butterfly), jps/Shutterstock; 23 (butterfly), Roger Meerts/Shutterstock; 23 (pupa), Jose B. Ruiz/NPL; 23 (egg), Silvia Reiche/MP; 23 (caterpillar), PeJo/Shutterstock; 24 (butterfly), Roger Meerts/Shutterstock; 24 (pupa), Jose B. Ruiz/NPL; 24 (egg), Silvia Reiche/MP; 24 (caterpillar), PeJo/Shutterstock; 24 (butterfly, bottom), jps/Shutterstock

Printed in the United States of America
16/WOR/2

ANSWER:

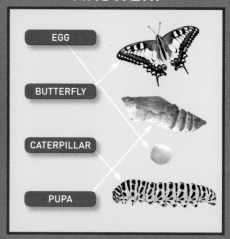

EGG

BUTTERFLY

CATERPILLAR

PUPA

National Geographic supports K–12 educators with ELA Common Core Resources. Visit natgeoed.org/commoncore for more information.